How It Turned Out

How It Turned Out

Selected Poems of Frank Redpath

Edited by John Wakeman

First Published in 1996
THE RIALTO
32 Grosvenor Road Norwich NR2 2PZ

ISBN: 0 9527444 0 6

The publisher acknowledges the financial assistance of the Esmée Fairbairn Charitable Trust and the Eastern Arts Board.

Eastern Arts Board Funded

Printed by Printing Services (Norwich) Ltd.

Twenty of these poems are reprinted, with Ted Tarling's generous permission, from Frank Redpath's first book, *To the Village*, published in 1986 by Tarling's Sonus press. Some previously appeared in Douglas Dunn's Hull anthology, *A Rumoured City* (Bloodaxe, 1982) or in magazines, among them The Rialto, Bête Noire, Wave, and Encounter.

Contents

INTRODUCTION

Critics are much given to affirming or denying the importance of this or that writer; to establishing maps of influence and lines of succession; to trying to separate what simply exists from what is likely to live. Frank Redpath (1927-90) would seem a prime candidate for this kind of treatment, although he never asserted his rights to it and has not so far received it. One might add that his patchy publishing history has almost prevented him having the chance to be underrated. Redpath, to a degree that would be almost inexplicable to the Darwinian young poets of today, was a good deal more interested in writing poems than in publicizing his existence. The world responded accordingly.

I hope this selection from his life's work will finally bring him the readership his fine, skilful, thoughtful poems deserve.

Coming from Hull, and spending much of his life there, Redpath can hardly avoid being associated with the work and supposed influence of Philip Larkin. Yet Redpath himself was surprised by the suggestion that his poems were coloured by Larkin's; and Redpath's friend and publisher Ted Tarling records a row across the dinner table, during which Redpath called Larkin "a political ignoramus" – which seems about right. There are similarities in their work, for example a way of combining an elaborate formality with vernacular wit; or the habit (now largely vanished) of treating poetry as a form of empirical enquiry. But their differences seem rather greater. Most strikingly, Redpath's work has none of the underlying nihilism from which Larkin's poetry seems to grow. Nor does he exhibit Larkin's odd blend of compassion and contempt: Redpath is respectfully curious, though at times very funny, about his fellow travellers in time. He can be pessimistic, but he is continually fascinated by people and life in general, and grateful, as Larkin was often unable to be, for any inspiriting occasion. Redpath's love poem, "Lyric", illustrates this. The speaker watches a woman putting on her make-up at the dressing-table:

Give me just this, he thought, let me for ever
Be sitting here with this, without a thought.
Ice ages come to freeze the flowing river,
Still ponds surround us both to cool the drought.
    Taking each eye in turn, she painted it
    Using a brush, a block of black, and spit.

The combination of fluency and decisive sentence structures, of romantic elegance and matter-of-factness, recalls MacNeice, whose "Meeting-Point" is perhaps audible in the background. And as with MacNeice, the surface colour of the work leads the reader (and the listener: Redpath deserves to be read aloud) towards the durable satisfactions of shape and craft.

Redpath shows great curiosity about form and his strong structural sense is also evident in less traditional-seeming poems, such as the exhilarating, wryly-titled "From Our Cycling Correspondent", where his work's recurrent sense of possibility is both the subject and part of the poem's dramatic form.

Two walls still stand, an arch,
in damp cold air. They say
You are here, it is now

But not still, time is passing.
Smoke rises from ceiling joists wigwammed
Over low piles of fallen bricks.

They burn. Flames excite themselves. The air
Shivers around them. They hurry
To tell themselves the news: we shall burn forever.

Down long broad avenues, crowds run
To greet the new Shah. Explosions and laughter.
They are picnicking on the barricades.

The economy is remarkable, and Redpath sacrifices none of his habitual clarity in this imaginative flight from familiar copulae to a new way of looking. The poem might be called mysteriously lucid, and its imaginative openness reveals something in common with some of his younger colleagues – such as Peter Didsbury and Douglas Houston – among the Hull poets chosen by Douglas Dunn for the anthology *A Rumoured City*.

What may even today haunt the work of the under-published poet is the term "provincial": here, as elsewhere, with his combination of technical attention and imaginative reach, Redpath disposes of the implied charge. He would certainly have understood Patrick Kavanagh's much quoted remark from "Epic": "Gods make their own importance." Poetry, that is to say, happens wherever the imagination is engaged. Many of Redpath's poems look at the lives of ordinary streets or the unremarkable yet seductive countryside of Holderness, or other bits of unoccupied England. The accidental and the seen-in-passing become markers for a way of life, and an attitude to it, which are carefully distinguished from the quaintness they are sometimes confused with. Hardy and Edward Thomas stand behind such work, but the writing is more than "school of":

> You have to learn a litany of signs
> To get you there in one:
> The broken barrow and the stack of churns,
> The disused harrow on
> The roadside where you meet the unmarked fork.
> Unplanned, impermanent. Odd that they work.
>
> "To the Village"

It is particularly interesting to read this (the title poem of the one collection Redpath published in his lifetime) alongside the violently contrasting "Transit Camp". The juxtaposition shows, for example, how un-evasive a poet Redpath was when he enjoyed what Douglas Dunn calls "the pleasant side of history". Almost inaudibly formal at first, "Transit Camp" carries rhymes across its long-lined stanzas of seemingly casual reminiscence. It may be fiction, or an episode from National Service; but whatever the exact period, the subject is, in Thom Gunn's phrase, "part, still, of the done war." It can certainly stand with most poetry of the Second World War. At some points, it seems prophetic of C.K. Williams – the long line, the concentration on the spoken and speaking detail, the sense that resistance to coming to the point is in fact functional – though the imagination is wholly Redpath's own. It's an account of a halt in the middle of nowhere in the middle of the night in bad weather. A troop train disgorges its men to stand about, eat sodden rations, march to improvised billets and in immemorial fashion speculate helplessly about what's going on. The material is familiar enough: it can be found, from an officer's perspective, in Waugh and Anthony Powell, and its record of powerlessness has something in common with Alun Lewis's "All Day It Has Rained", or Julian McClaren-Ross's "I Went Sick", or any number of accounts of being on the wrong end of military mushroom theory. Part of Redpath's contribution is to make the poem's readers, like the narrator and his fellow-soldiers, the victims of hearsay and incompleteness:

> And after a bit, the noises started: a sort of tight
> Screeching sound from the trolleys, then something clanging.
> Once somebody inside yelled *Keep it moving on the right!*
> And we could hear this shuffling sound and something banging.
> There were pipes, jutting out overhead, that kept on spurting
> Jets of steam, and a smell that was sort of shitty and flat.

It's a fine dramatic piece of writing, whose grimmer suggestions – for example that this is how men might grow used to the idea that atrocity has nothing to do with them and is thus thinkable – remain restlessly in the mind. I would want to read this poem alongside those of Louis Simpson, Randall Jarrell and Keith Douglas, for its sense of what it's like to live on the unsignposted interior of history.

Between the publication of *To the Village* in 1986 and his death in 1990, Redpath's work entered a particularly fruitful period – prompted, perhaps, by the awareness that his illness meant time was short. Yet the seizing of the days produced poems where the fascination with life remained emphatic. "Marked Changes" (June 1988) about a spell in hospital, has death calmly if soberly in prospect, but retains its curiosity, foregoes no useful detail. "Humber (2)" (1st November 1987), reads the river as history, and time as the element which strips us of the imaginative power of childhood. Yet the poem's necessary paradox is revealed in the effortless evocation of the river disappearing like "a road into/ strange midland distances". Paradoxical too, and among the most impressive of the late pieces is "Unstressed Areas" (published in *Bête Noire* in Spring 1988). It's a poem with particular meanings to those who've lived in Hull in the postwar period, watching its seemingly immutable bombsites and wild gardens brought finally to commercial book; but it also, I think, speaks more generally for the radical, generous and much-betrayed generation whose youth was defined by the war and the years immediately after:

> ... Vistas will soon give way to making a living.
> But not for me. From now on I shall please
>
> Myself, and chart these unattended stations:
> Corners where old could-have-been-othernesses
> Amble, unthreatening, into the now-and-seen
> To wear embarrassed grins and tattered dresses
> And offer, as on dancing-floors, joined celebrations
> Of all that was with all that might have been.

This provides a reminder of why we like poetry, of how lines and stanzas come back unbidden to mind at ordinary moments – on a train, on a walk, or looking through a window. The knowledge, tactfully and movingly indicated in these lines, that there are things only poetry can say, seems to have been Frank Redpath's reason for writing. May this book enable many more readers to share what has so far been the prized experience of a few.

Sean O'Brien

From "October 20, 1990"
For Frank Redpath

A walk in Pearson Park, you showed us
where Larkin lived and watched –
like the trees, long-time used to loss –
spring arriving, new flowers toss.
I see you receding there, fag in hand,
the slow sure step; out of sight before
the cold lights have to come on at four
at the end of another year.
I will put my arm in yours where you showed
us the unfear. . . .

Rhiannon Wakeman

Cover painting: 'Pearson Park' by Ted Tarling

Landscapes

To walk on warm, packed, quilted earth and smell
Crushed thyme, hear whirrings in the grass
On a forward slope in the sun, then pass
By woodland and some disused, narrow-gauge
Rails to an overgrown canal, its towpath well
Baffled by briars but still with some
Forceable ways to The Works – an unroofed cage
For bits of engines and the paint-peeling, pine
Cubby the clerk used, windows watching dunes –
Has always made me think, "This could be home."

Evacuated for the war, I used to play
In Early-Auden country every Saturday.
I hadn't read him, then, but loved it anyway.

And here, before that Whitsun, any train
That smelt of carriages and slowed to meet
Existing silence at a halt, clanked on, some feet,
Then stopped, then made a fuss, then started once again,
I knew was safe, yet somehow sad, humane;
A purchasable, advantageous goldfish-bowl
Outside which, home would grow – allotments, then
Gliding across, the streets; the tea-time city
Self-absorbed, unconscious; unconcerned with me,
Those men on corners, reading the Sports Mail.

The house where Larkin lived, that peers across
The trees in Pearson Park, though long-time-used to loss,
Watched and still watches Spring arrive, new flowers toss.

Perhaps all poets do is make a case
For ways of being we already know
Already love or fear. They do it nimbly, though,
And what responds in us is what is glad
It's not alone, that in whatever place
It makes itself there'll be another voice
To say it's not unlicensed or gone mad.
Landscapes are common ground, lie outside time
And reassure you that you're not to blame
Entirely, being somehow born with, like your name.

Coming To

Remembering purpose suddenly, hearing the clock,
Is always to be lifted from that sailing
Utterly unintentioned elsewhere; looking,
Feel, between tick and yes-I-thought-so tick,
Frank recognition wheedling you to share
Whatever reach-me-down events surround you there.

Always a shock, but it soon passes. Why,
There's Mrs. Body-Language from Dun Brown
Taking her dogs out for a crap; that clown
Who always parks his car with one wheel high
Mounting the kerb; lumping from tree to tree,
That lass who jogs and jogs so earnestly.

It seems to fill their time. Why shouldn't he
Who sits here, vacant in a cooling car,
Get out and do as they do? Check the doors,
March up the path, go in and make some tea?
He will. He always has. But not without, untrained,
The sense of some huge ocean being drained,

Some timeless tide retreating, leaving the pier
Grey, mussel-crusted, drying; tilted smacks
Newly defined and useless; weathered rocks
Disarmed, reduced to holding rock-pools; gear
For loading, launching, signalling left dry:
And more time left than these can justify.

Miss White

Chaps of my age, who've learnt it's better to
Stay fast asleep, half-wake at night and go
Fumbling along the landing to the loo;
Don't switch the light on, sit to have a pee,
Lean on the opened door edge: so,
Try to preserve insensibility.

It never worked: the thin white cat would hear,
Who slept, long-legged and awkward, on the stair.

Aloof by day, a stalking elegance
Who rarely purred, but sometimes would bestow
Favour upon my knee and butt my chin,
What I'll miss now is that surprising ghost
Who'd march in there to join me, climb into
My dropped pyjama trousers, make a nest.

Absurd familiar I named Miss White,
Gone, now, taking your gift: laughter at night.

Dilemma

Yellow and purple and white
And green – and a green, and a green . . . .
And already the moment is past
As I look at what I've seen
And the yellow forms into blots
That move above the green.

Pansies are they? Or poppies?
And two sorts of ... hanging bells?
So the itch arrives, and the shame
Of not knowing what most know well
And wanting to label and name
Which is, wanting to buy and sell.

But how else can I look,
See dark-veined petals hold
The morning light in cups
Shaken on stalks, see bold
Rank upon rank stand up
Of blade and leaf, nor be told

That *look* is the death of *see*?
Only by taking care
Can I measure that feathered space
Between past and future, where
Presence is taking place
On the edge of that petal there.

Short Story

When Stone, the spy, came down from the hill
Past Danby's stack-yard and over the stile,
He wandered around like a summer visitor
Then settled in Carlo's café by the harbour.
He was spotted right off: all knew who he was.
Nobody liked to be awkward; nobody made a fuss.

He stayed there for years. Never had much to say –
"Good night," of course, "Good morning,"
      – he'd pass the time of day.
Never seemed short of money, but got a job on the pier;
People who came in the summer thought he was born there.
One of the locals married him; said he was always polite,
So she left him for somebody lively. He stayed quiet.

Then one night he got drunk. Started to rant and rave,
"I was up on that hill for years, I watched your every move.
I lay in a fold in the frozen rock with my Zeiss binoculars,
I crawled down close to your walls and listened
      under the summer stars
I wrote my reports: they brought me food.
      Don't go asking who.
And don't go thinking you know me,
      because I'm the one who knows you."

Bilious stuff. Nobody minded. Next day he was gone.
Romantics said, "Recalled to the hall of an elsewhere baron
Who paid him a pittance to watch." When they went to look
They found a rotted sleeping-bag up in the folded rock.
His, maybe. People picnic there,
      don't think it time to change;
Though the tea-time town when they return
      may seem a trifle strange.

Eden in the Avenues

From where we sit, our garden is
A well-worn phrase of green and green.
A close inspection of the grass
Shows it is "dappled," though what's seen
Between these walls of "matured brick"
Is, some would say, house-agent's rhetoric.

So neatly here is your eye led
By arbour, fish-pool, rose-bush, lawn
To soft-fruit patch and potting-shed,
It's hard to think that we who own
This imitation space, this rustic dream,
Could ever be less wholesome than we seem.

Our lusts, you see, are small. Some say
We hide them well. We envy few
Who haven't done as well as we.
Anger, when costly, we eschew.
We're seldom slothful. None of us will shirk
The job of telling you how hard we work.

When meeting us, you quickly learn
That we are horrified by greed –
We know what dockers ought to earn.
Quite properly, we're only proud
Of what we've done. Intemperate and brimming
Gluttony we keep at bay by slimming.

Alas, our garden is a plot.
These ordered spaces put a face
On fact: that what we do may not
Be nice. We have our little ways,
And each commits these seven sins at least –
And, eighth and worst,
    we're well in with the priest.

Palm

Easter again, my grandfather would ask
The chemist for a bag of logwood chips,
Boil them with half-a-dozen big white eggs.
Fire, water, mystery. A yearly task.

Deliberately performed, always the same,
It gave him in due course six heavy, smooth
Indigo-violet bombs, solid and dark,
Which then were left to cool. Half job, half game.

What was it pleased him? What I watched, for me,
Was something he just knew how to do. It seemed
Unlikely he had a father, being so old,
Or that he'd had to learn his alchemy.

Act Two began with steel. The smaller blade
He thumbnailed from his knife was, I believed,
The sharpest in the world. With it he'd scratch
White lines on the dark shells until he'd made

Four curving willow twigs that we called Palm,
Thick with alternate leaves, enclosing two
Dark oval spaces, one marked with the date,
The other, florid capitals: my name.

We didn't value them. Admired for
A day or two at most, his careful work
Always got cracked. The eggs made a small feast.
It didn't matter; next year there'd be more.

Free Water

To see rain-water fill a butt – home to
Small curlicues that looked alive, but weren't –
Under a lean-to roof, spilled through
A cracked black pipe and gutter-growths of fern
Always seemed so safe: symbol of taking care,
Provision for a drought. The country-women said
Nothing could beat its softness for your face and hair.

In rained-on streets, tall fall-pipes jewelled out
Across the flags, skeined plattering cascades
Which wonderfully ran to waste.
I fantasised deep cisterns, dark arcades
Beneath the streets where treasure would be found,
Viz: grating-swallowed bracelets, wedding rings,
    small coins.
Not wasted: dripping bricks pooled mystery underground.

Both, preparation for that wild, unmeasured gift,
Endured, not loved at first; knobbed cobbles,
    moorland track
Battered by rain until deep rifts
Formed on the forward slope, and spouts drained back
The way you'd come, pointing to where, ahead,
You'd maybe reach unguaranteed reward:
Somewhere to walk wind-dried, dry-shod. A watershed.

Miss Er

We walked, as I remember, towards a sandpit,
Across a field that was 'heavily endowed'
(I was heavily into elegant speech in those days)
With cowpats. Can't remember: was there cloud,
Or clouds, or the usual Humberside haze?

Remember it well. Thing is I can't remember
What she was wearing, only I know that what
She was wearing was something that seemed important.
There was a lane, I remember, and . . . yes, it was hot,
Or muggy certainly . . . and dredging equipment –

That I'm almost certain of – parked by a hedge.
But this about Miss Er I do recall: she said
Every time I come out with you, I get filthy dirty –
Half laughing, of course, and . . . tossing her head?
To be truthful, only the words, after thirty-

Odd years, come back – words and how it felt
To be so worried and pleased, to be dazzled
That she'd 'deigned' to notice me, that I was puzzled
And nervous wondering what she meant.

Post-War Credit

1

Called to endure the raid, we make
Accustomed moves in darkness, dress
(Have lain half-dressed already), speak
No more than names, answer no more than *yes*,
Cross the black room and reach the landing. Light
Waves from a lifted candle there, restoring sight.

How expertly we move. The shadows reel
Of blanket-bundled, caped-in-coverlet
Mutterers down the dark stairwell wall.
Comfort is any word that's definite,
Inaccurate or not. That steady drone
Is one of ours, those thunder-claps our own

Guns we can place and call by name. Yet, when
Loud undeniable disaster very near
Asserts itself, belief's not shattered. At once
New doctrine (out into the shelter where
All may be saved) is obvious. We know
No word but *now*, have no concern but *go*.

This dispensation starts with plaster underfoot
And a jammed door to scrabble at and jerk
Free of its hinges in the stink of soot.
Outside, bright cloud-reflected, unrebuked
Firelight – that's *one* good thing – to show the way
Past men amazingly at work with hoses. "Bright as day,

You could have read a book, it was that clear,"
We'll tell it, later, but now, incurious,
Hurry to dripping concrete darkness, where
Reports are brought by one ridiculous
Hero who steps inside to light a fag and tell
Traveller's tales of what goes ill, what well.

2

All clear. Short sleep. The dead have been tidied away,
The unlucky have been ordered back to work
And we, the newly homeless, sent on holiday.

It must be holiday. Rules about public undress
Were relaxed in the place where we waited; tea was brought
In tall white jugs, and the bread they brought was less

Formally sliced than the bread we have at home.
We have travelled in buses with strangers, and strangers
Have found us somewhere to sleep and taken away our names.

Anonymous now, and thinking we know what's what,
Not one yet understands what time will show:
That we have been at school all day, and got

Our lesson off by heart, that nothing will ever be sure
Ever again. Unlike the stupid dead, we've earned
A kind of bootleg freedom kit. It's worn
Next to the skin, unmentioned, treasured for years.

After Dunkirk

All units of the O.T.C.
Parade at oh-nine-hundred hours.
The older boys, who wear puttees
And First-War uniforms are thrown
Into a ring inside the town,
Where, armed with bags of powdered chalk,
They wait to meet invading hordes
Of the next village's Home Guard.

Two members of the Lower School
In blazers, worn with service caps,
Are sent to stand out on patrol.
Their disappointing orders are
To watch, report, not open fire.
Equipped with message-pads and maps
And warned they must not lurk in barns
They settle down in a green lane.

After the first attentive hour,
One of them lights a cigarette;
The other shares it. When a car
First heard a mile away drones past,
They lie in a machine-gun nest
And blast it over open sights.
Unharmed, it sighs away; the sun
Climbs on, the exercise is done.

Relieved, they trail back through the town
To hear a battle has been fought
Outside the shut-down Odeon
And won by the right side. Tall tales
Are licenced and grow taller still.
Reports are made. Time now to eat,
Then, back to duty to decide
What England then has now been made.

The War-Cemetery, Brouay

Certain events took place, and History
Records them safely in the book. What's here
But modest warehousing, a list of names?

Half-interested, the summer visitor
May note the Ox and Bucks must have been caught
In something nasty, half-way through July.

But now, the pregnant silence of that hill
Hides nothing here but pleasure, and before
Is picture-postcard country where we can be safe.

So where is Gunner Mostyn Jenkins, aged eighteen,
Born somewhere in Glascoed, Monmouthshire
And buried here in earth? The stone,
Like every Gunner's, mentions everywhere.

How dare I weep? How dare I stand, and cry?

Transit Camp

. . . came to a place – funny – I felt I half remembered,
With some sort of shed or factory, on the farther side
Of a cinder track by the railway siding, with dismembered
Bits of machinery, being rained on, dumped outside.
Blank walls, sliding doors,windows blacked out with
        metal sheeting,
Unpainted and greasy, welded to angle-iron frames.

Well, they got us off, lined us up, got the names
Of our units, then gave the usual order: stand over there
        and wait.
No idea where we were, of course; been some sort of fun
        and games
Back down the line; they'd taken the officers off. It was late
When we got there, pitch black, pissing down. The only
        lighting
Was three lamps on poles. It looked like the arsehole of hell.

After a bit, they sent up rations and somebody to tell
Us to carry on waiting. Rations! A mess-tin half full of tea
That tasted like yesterday's warm-up, and a wad that was
        well
Soaked in the pissing-down rain; we ate it lined up in the lee
Of the wall. Then somebody opened a door and I got a
        fleeting
Glimpse inside: a dozen blokes, big bastards, Staff,
        I suppose,

Clearing up after a shift it looked like. One was coiling a
hose
And the rest were sweeping up some sort of muck from
the floor,
Stripped to the waist, wearing oilskin aprons. There were
rows
Of flat-bed trolleys on trackways that went across to a door
In the far wall. The bloke said *Fuck! Still fucking raining*,
Then slammed the door shut again. We waited there half
the night

And, after a bit, the noises started: a sort of tight
Screeching sound from the trolleys, then something clanging.
Once somebody inside yelled *Keep it moving on the right!*
And we could hear this shuffling sound and something
banging.
There were pipes, jutting out overhead, that kept on spurting
Jets of steam, and a smell that was sort of shitty and flat.

Then some sort of officer came up in a car and told us that
We shouldn't be where we were and marched us five
bloody miles,
Down the track, through a wood, with the officer sat on
his fat
Arse in the car in front, to some huts. They gave us piles
Of straw and sacks to sleep on but we weren't complaining;
We'd have slept on the floor, by then, to be out of the rain.

Three bloody days they kept us there. We kept hearing
the train
Whistling in the distance but nobody could tell us where
We were supposed to be. Nothing but rumours, no plain
Answers: *It's nothing to do with us; we're not going there;*
We're moving on tomorrow; somebody said it's a home
posting.
Still, you can get used to just about anything. Anyway . . .

Conclusions

"The evil stumble and fall
And die in strange places." Or so
It's told at one in the lonely
As the late-night T.V. show
Murders its villain and ends.

Or else, "I love you." "And I
Love you," and the camera's winched
Away, to leave them tiny
In a miles-wide, fourteen inch
Forever of flowers and light.

Don't laugh. Such certainties
Are comfort when stairs and the dark
Beckon, and unwashed cups
Are all you can pledge to mark
Some sort of faith in tomorrow.

And, outside all, the night
Aches over Humberside
As a wind made of empty tins
And iron roofing rides
Bare-arsed by rusting docks

Where all you can learn is that life
Is mostly leaving behind
Things you had wit to start
But never could finish, to find
More things, whose meaning you
Can't fathom or know to be true.

Humber (2)

It slides beneath our dreams:
Through spaces left between
The timbers of the pier,
Children on hold-hand walks
Safe on a giant floor
Watched something uncaring
Muscle its way past piles
And, fifteen feet below,
Saw glints and roils and gleams.

Later, adventuring
On ferry, barge or shore,
Thought only that it brought
Timber, bananas, cod;
Or shone, a road into
Strange midland distances
Where people went to work
In factories they'd seen
On soap or cocoa tins.

Grown like our parents now,
Less often do we sleep
Deeply enough to reach
That skin, where our lives bob
An inch or two above
All that it carries off:
Dung, cattle-trodden ways,
Farms, grain by grain, and wolds
And chalk: old skeletons.

Tinker, Tiler . . .

Something is prancing, up where nothing should
Be moving but slow end-of-winter cloud.
An ape upon a roof-top scaffold would
Be worth a glance but, when I stop, the high
Surprising farce becomes a commonplace:
A roof man at his work. Who would look twice?
Petrouchka, in grey overalls, against the sky.

A silent yelp, down from his here-today-
And-gone-tomorrow theatre, must have
Sparked the ground crew. A pulley starts to play,
Whirls, stops and hurls a bucket, on a line,
Into his waiting hands. Insouciant,
He slops it in a barrow and it's sent
Swooping for more. A moral lesson here? A sign?

Perhaps not. But looking up I see the birds:
Grey trills and ornaments along a crest.
They share what he endures: a quite absurd
Hold on the thin edge of the everyday . . .
And dangerous too, for when they fly how quick
They're hurled – and he; no matter how you look
You'll get a wink, no more, before they're gone. So,

Forty years on, remember how I learned –
Unwillingly – to dig a decent ditch,
And now am glad that I can say I earned
My living with a graft, knew how to slice
Unbroken slabs of turf, mark out a cant
And throw the first spoil wide so it would mount
Into a stable heap around my working space.

Chapel Band

Some huge, forthcoming triumph, we
On nodding terms with angels in the street;
Arthritis banished, all the lame set free. . .
Details would be adjustable: the sound,
Blown on assorted silver elephants,
Would not. It would be round

All round, and somehow shining, yet
Not just for show; it would be nourishing
Like holy soup supped through your ears: the feet
Of everyone who heard would have small wings
So they could fly while upright, as in dreams.
They blew: we heard. No things

Left uneuphonicked, we, the band
Then parted, met outside. Some ferried back
Unlikely, solid-seeming cases, and
Some smoked like mortal men, while we, as they
Trekked home through Sunday-evening silence in
Late sunlight, turning grey.

From Our Cycling Correspondent

Biking to work was a good idea. Improbable insects
Of giant yellow steel have been at work
For weeks among the slums.

They have cleared whole squares of houses, shops,
Small factories where lives were made, and furtive
Embraces. Light has been let in.

Don't jump to conclusions. List
What you can see. Here
Was some kind of an enclosure.

Two walls still stand, an arch,
In damp cold air. They say
You are here, it is now

But not still, time is passing.
Smoke rises from ceiling joists wigwammed
Over low piles of fallen bricks.

They burn. Flames excite themselves. The air
Shivers around them. They hurry
To tell themselves the news: we shall burn forever.

Down long broad avenues, crowds run
To greet the new Shah. Explosions and laughter.
They are picnicking on the barricades.

Unstressed Areas

Fallen, largely, into disuse, still falling
As new importances arrange themselves about
Such stubborn ghosts as live in dereliction,
My city offers new and transient delights.
There are such corners here among the rusting
And here proliferate much-needed fictions.

Take, for example, that new-founded
Empire of willow-herb and celandine
Along two foundry walls, still in their places:
The rest has gone. Now you can see, between
Old furnace-beds and over them, unbounded
Spaces that once were working privacies.

Not fanciful to think of something waiting
For this short time to be. New walls are planned,
And builders' pegs are planted: some will cross
Old roads where few would want to walk now, and
Vistas will soon give way to making a living.
But not for me. From now on I shall please

Myself, and chart these unattended stations:
Corners where old could-have-been-othernesses
Amble, unthreatening, into the now-and-seen
To wear embarrassed grins and tattered dresses
And offer, as on dancing-floors, joined celebrations
Of all that was with all that might have been.

Knitting

Making a map out of string, you could knot
A Turk's head for Hull,
Surround it with various nets, make a blot
Of the right size for Swanland, another for Aike,
And so on, and so on. Rolled in a ball,
It would look pretty odd, though compact. To make
A decision while driving, you'd spread it on your knee
And tell it without looking, like a sort of rosary.

Fingered, it would be full of holes, and so
The usual, flat,
Cartographer's lie, which suggests there are no
Places you can't drive to, wouldn't work
However thin your string. More truthful, that,
And very much safer, too. The dark
Spaces you see between the rows of lights
Are well-known haunts of giants and similar frights.

Safe journeys then, stringfellows! But take care:
Towns may be crocheted, but that's
No guarantee of safety, any year;
Walls rise and fall so fast they flicker, and
No net you knit will catch them. What's
There all the time? Ah, neither wind nor rain
Which any fool photographer can trap,
But light without place, unmarked on any map.

To the Village

Everyone, I suspect, learns his own way
To find the place: though most
Leave the main road by the transport café
Then head towards the coast,
The signposts in the by-ways are erratic,
Their placings local, idiosyncratic.

Some quite important turnings are not named;
Some that look promising
End up in paddocks or deserted farms
Or lead you in a ring
Fingered by names that don't turn into places
Through narrowing hedge-vistas with no houses.

You have to learn a litany of signs
To get you there in one:
The broken barrow and the stack of churns,
The disused harrow on
The roadside where you meet the unmarked fork.
Unplanned, impermanent. Odd that they work.

Journeys

For Mary

Home before dark: three hundred capsuled miles
Of Wales and England lie behind. Later,
They'll be reduced in memory stew into
One journey: often made, and melded. Even
The toyshop in Machynlleth and the pee
We never had in shut-down Mold will swim
Undated in a celebrated sometimes-when.

So with our Christmas jaunts to Southminster:
Teas at the Black-and-White, the Great North Road,
Alconbury Hill, and then the plunge into
Huntingdonshire and Essex, plugging through
Small market towns with lighted shops and snow
(The plastic kind) drifted in every window
And people buying trees and doing well.

For years we kept a blanket, stitched a badge
For every town we visited. The rule
Was, "If we stopped there long enough for tea."
Somebody washed it, cockled all the braid.
We gave up doing it, and took instead
To sandwiches and vacuum flasks and breaks
At odd, unlikely spots in woods, by lakes.

The journeys of a married lifetime coin
Small change to trade with friends – "We always used. . ."
Or, "When the kids were young. . ." Good table-fun.
Like goldfish in a bowl we hardly see
Our water: Mobilopolis. Grandad
Took to it like a duck in Thirty-three,
In Crossley, Riley Nine or Austin Ten.

Such innocence. Long journeys then involved
Some time with maps and tools the day before,
And people still could think, "the car that goes
So far..." – a blameless badge that you belonged
To those who'd won a battle decently.
But things go faster now. The roads are fraught
With strips of torn-off tread from juggernauts,

And every lay-by's now an ad-hoc bog
Where people dump half-eaten burgers, chips
And cola cans, and exercise the dog
Briefly, when it's relieved itself. Not nice.
And Christmas Eve, in two opposing roars,
Wales-London, London-Wales, the faithful pour
To reach their dears at ninety miles an hour.

Was the cup always poisoned? History says
As many died in nineteen-thirty-six
From using cars as now. Oh, well, I think
We drink because we need the nourishment
That's brewed from setting-out to getting there;
The sense that we're in charge of time and space
That's safer, too, than living in one place.

Safer: we hope that no official map
Has the co-ordinates to make that world
We travelled through into a target. No
Outsider can get in without our say-so.
So if I say, "The horse-shoe pass half-way,"
Or "Where red bricks begin as you go North,"
I'm speaking of events, and what they're worth

To no-one else but us and those we love,
Imperfectly, with tears. Leaving is larks,
Arriving shrugs. "Good journey?" "Pretty fair,
It cleared up after Grantham." So, I give
This as my true belief: between was where
I'm glad to say we've been, and were at most alive.

Between the Frames

When I wrote for kids' comics, I had lists
Inside my head: What Our Readers Like –
A hero, solving problems with his fists
And winning races on his motor-bike;

Two snarling villains, pouring oil in pools
At Dangerous Corner, which our Jack will miss
By swerving up that track which they, the fools,
Have failed to notice: but, a precipice. . . .

Writing such stuff, where things that were too wet
To make a picture fell between the frames,
Referred to, if at all, as "Later. . .", set
Above the next exploding fun and games,

It's not surprising that I came so late
To see *between the frames* was mostly how
My life would mostly fall; later, to celebrate
That dispensation; and now

Always to cry "*Later*? Go back! Let's *see*
Old Jackie peeling spuds, warming the pot;
Let's learn just what his sister's kid, aged three,
Did when the next-door neighbour called
        and most exactly what,
In greatest detail, mind, the next-door neighbour did
        and said,"
Belay that "*Later*," chum. Later we'll all be dead.

Edge-On

As it is in dreams,
When you can never be sure
Who is telling the story, or
Quite, what seems
To be the point of view,

So that, unpuzzled, you
Move from the face-to-face
Real me, real somebody else
To a film you're sitting through,
Or a document on T.V.

Which creates, at monstrous cost,
An authentic-seeming now
With well-known actors who play
Parts they have lived in the past
In sets not built to last. . .

So may seem the busiest, long,
Inconsequentially shaped
Time between waking and sleep,
When loss that is wildly wrong
Becomes, "Really? Well, of course. . . ."

Notes for a Life

He had an eye for country, always could
Look over level fields with not one fence,
Know they were scored across by hidden dykes.
The tempting sunken roads some found, that sped
Down between sunlit dunes, he saw at once
Were all dead ends, led quickly into brakes.

His habit grew, of waiting by the car.

We never found the beach, it got too late.
We found an old cement works though, and went
Exploring there. That road along the dune
Was overgrown with brambles; you were right.
We ate about a pound apiece. They weren't
Quite ripe but not too bad. How have you been?

Later report suggests that he grew deaf.

Cornered

What he says in the pub
Means nothing, but he keeps on trying.
To show you, snaps are spread:
A man knelt in a cornfield, years ago;
He gestured at the camera; a girl
Smiled over her shoulder; some others, lolling,
Looked up and grinned at what he said;
One with her back to you unpacked the grub.

What he can tell you here
He knows is uninformative: jobs, names,
What one was famous for.
You think it must have been a royal pain
Hearing about their pranks, but he insists
It wasn't that . . . not just the fun and games . . .
Just . . . when you live like that, you know the score.
His tongue goes lame. He reaches for his beer.

What is there you can say?
He traps you with his fat man's sit, spread knees.
Cold comfort to be told
Some lives, all maybe, go that way. God knows
How small the stock was he's been living on!
Don't say you understand; he won't be pleased.
He wants what you can't give: to know the gold
Lattice of summer will come back one day.

Say that you have to go,
Make an excuse and leave, head for the Gents,
For if you've understood
What's eating this old fool it's not because
Of how he bent your ear but what you've seen.
For him, that hoard of brief exposures meant
Fear. When that summer stopped, it stopped for good.
His words were meant to hide it. Better go.

Clever Lad

I saw a child hold up his finger:
He lifted up his finger and pointed at the sun.
The finger sprouted leaves and spread out branches.
A potent sort of child, if ever I saw one.

Then he dreamed up a tree and a square around it,
A sort of London square: rather posh, rather old,
With cars parked by the railings and quiet houses,
As the sun went down and lights came on and it turned cold

And two people in a doorway quarrelled and parted;
One went off and the other went in.
Someone slammed a car-door, someone laughed
out loud in the evening
As he walked off in a hurry, angry as hell and arguing.

Then a light came on in an upstairs window and she sat
Nursing her knees on her bed, and staring
At the wall that remembered his shadow, and wondering
Just what had bitterly got into him, to make him act like that.

And when you come to think of it, what right had he
to argue?
He had it the way he wanted it, didn't he? Still,
Maybe he was a bit young when he dreamed up his garden.
You can't blame a child if it's got less sense than will.

But he shouldn't have done what he did: hopped
over the railings
And chopped down the tree, to leave her without any shade.
He'll regret it all right, when he sees how the railings
have lengthened
And he finds himself trapped in the hot little world
that he made.

Comparative

Are many kinds of good –
Packing, driving a car
From a friend's house through woods
To a friend's house, and there,
Having good news to tell,
Finding their lives go well.

All tend to that one best,
That landfall made alone,
Where no-one takes the least
Notice, and you are one
More accident, no more,
On that rewarding shore

Where all are busy; some
Making a chum of death;
Some wrist-watching the time
From breath to breath, beneath
That sun whose obscure art
Makes them apart, a part.

New Year Visit

F*or John and Hilary Wakeman*

Spring crops have candlewicked the fields
And big-wheel tractors ruled straight ledger-lines
Across their curving promise, hedge-to-hedge; behind
Black hill-crest farms and coppices, the sun's
Shared family fortune dips, five miles at most
Off to the west; it seems the sort of thing
That foundrymen could handle with long tongs.

The train that carries me to friends,
Though Sunday-service, runs to time, and in
The change-at station buffet – it's overwomanned
For five spaced, dreaming travellers – someone
Chunks a win on the bandit: there's a sense
Of competence relaxing, end-of-fuss,
And evening, eastern-edge-of-Englandness.

Norwich: lights came on early here,
Among the first to notice it grew dark,
And pass the news to Anglesey. I'm taxied where
I fall into a safety of old jokes.
Somebody's cleared a peg: grinning, I find
I'm drinking wine, amid a family din
Of news and questions, cooking, half-made plans.

What follows is delight: I fit
Into made spaces in two working lives
Who pick the New Year up in hope and faith, in spite
Of having seen new years grow old; I love
My friends well as I can, knowing I can't
Haunt everywhere, like Superman; my days
Are working, shopping, laughter, decency.

All visits end as pictures: one
Friend fills my glass and hands a book, marking
The place to read; one sails back on a bike, darts in
From some mysterious, early, churchy thing
For her quick second breakfast, with my first.
And, last, that kitchen-library-diner-thoroughfare
Filled suddenly with sons; a daughter with red hair.

Leaving, across the fens, I find
The year already growing usual.
Three boys get on at Ely, play short hands
Of cards; we change at Peterborough; I feel
That North-magnetic pull begin, and make
A list of things to do: of nineteen eighty-nine,
Three hundred, I hope, and sixty doing days remain.

How It Turned Out

One I imagined standing on a dark hill, with the lights
        of the city before him,
A sign grown into his hand, a directing pressure
        between his eyes;
Not to be fooled with mirrors,thorn-cruel maybe, but vital;
Soon to be shown a dark world, yes, but brimming,
        a busy harbour
With houses lighted and open and dancing about the trees,
And a salesman's twist of the road through, roaring
        from friend to friend round lovely corners.

Was given instead a distorting-glass, a guide in
        broken English
And a sextant but no sun; only, repeatedly, morning
Greyly disgracing him. And, further, was denied
The ability to dance, the hieratic steps
Or the shrugging coward's posture, but was left
Alone on a long road, with a diminishing memory
        of North.

Information About Love

"... events with equal surprisal values may not be equally surprising to an observer." F. Attneave. "Applications of Information Theory to Psychology."

The message has redundancy, we say,
Whenever symbols or events occur
That are not equiprobable. The dear
Murmurs I love you to her darling lay.

Hardly surprising. We all lie in bed.
Would he have been more staggered if (her feet
Tucked happy round his happy shoulders), hate
You darling had been what she said?

Well, yes, he would. What's more, the theory goes,
Uncertainty reduces only when
What's done is unexpected. Nothing can
Be gained the second time he counts her toes.

So why's he worried? Could it be the fact
That while the theory works, for Heads and Tails,
When faced with counting bits in bed, he feels
Uncertainty increase with each new act?

What fun for us! He'll never realise
When madam whispers love you, more than half
The chances are she's talking to herself
And simply trying feelings on for size.

Lunar

Improbable as ever stands
The moon in mid-day blue, blue-shadowed, thinly gleaming,
Washed to a rag. How disturbing, still, that
Inappropriate presence, that unrelenting,
Wrong-time stare. It shouldn't watch us waking,
Busy with lawful business, rational demands.

The midnight sun would not be such
A questioner. Old northern friend who sags but stays
Up well beyond last knockings, it wouldn't mind
Shining while we slept on; it's natural to doze,
Knowing you'll wake to warmth. But that ironic gaze . . .
So this is what you get up to. Not much.

I've seen you skate well outside time, chat to the dead
Who weren't surprised to see you, or, uncaged
Monsters below, cling panting to a narrowing ledge
Then step through walls to safety. Tell me,
Doesn't it pall, this stroll to pay these bills,
This pop in for a cup, this light this fag, this café?

Eclipse

Beyond all the last lamps, the full moon. Parting,
"Can *you* see the hare in the moon?" I said, and she,
"Oh, did you know? There's an eclipse tonight." So, sorting
Through times in the paper we planned
    to watch it separately.

Most of us can't get too near to the big words. *Love*
For us is seeing someone look *light* for a moment,
    not Tristan
Sounding for years from a wide stage, or the dove
Scattering flame from its shivering wings. If we begin

To grizzle for that sort of thing we foozle it, likely as not
Invest in a last line of spiky conditions
    to keep surrender out,
Try to convince ourselves, hear ourselves lying: all that
Can end in a narrowing, sorry, bamboozled redoubt.

But: separately, two bodies at opposite ends of a pull
Watched our world shadow the shining. Elsewhere,
    a fore-advised
Friend with binoculars, deckchair and blanket plotted the full
Yarn from first bite to last glitter; but I, less organised,

Leaned on an elderly wall and smoked; went in,
    came out to see
Only (only!) what I'd forgotten: that it never quite goes away,
But leaves a sort of hole in the sky where something, patently,
Still goes on; a coppery light, some verdigris, a ray

Of unexpected sparkle from the almost-dark disc, reporting
How solidly it hangs, light or dark, seen or not, asserting
That gravity engendered, now and once, a necessary joining.

Story Time

I think that what she said
Involved being nineteen, away from home
To take some kind of test, an interview.
She met an older man, someone who knew
What it was all about, who gave her some
Lunch and some good advice but didn't try it on.

Later, I think, there was
A mix-up with the trains that made her late.
She thought that Deptford (Dartford, was it?) lay
Just down the line from where she had to stay
So trotted off there. Did I get this right?
Something quite frightening, then? A dog that
snatched her glove?

Disasters, more or less.
At least, I think they were. Remembering such
Details as these is not what I do best.
Partly that while she spoke, I held her breast
Cupped in my hand, partly the rich
Dazzle of what I thought I saw got in the way.

While she was talking I
Kept looking backwards at her in the train:
London approaching like brass instruments
Announcing the arrival of presents
While she prepared for freedom, on her own
In clothes she thought were splendid, and clean underwear.

We meet less often now.
Painful to limp up stairs we used to leap
Three at a time, but sometimes when we do
She holds a dress up. "Look at this, it's new.
Isn't it splendid?" When she does, I hope
That she will always be moving towards that good

She posed for years ago.
Therefore I send her this apology
For poor attention to her complex tales
And to explain that when she does her nails,
Looks round and catches me, and says, "Are you
Laughing at me?" and I say, "Yes" I mean, "Thank you."

Lyric

Something is happening that never, ever,
Happened to anyone before, he thought.
This is the moment when the sudden river
Breaks through the rocks to flow and end the drought.
  Sitting straight-backed upon the bedside chair,
  She took pins from her lips and fixed her hair.

Give me just this, he thought, let me for ever
Be sitting here with this, without a thought.
Ice ages come to freeze the flowing river,
Still ponds surround us both to cool the drought.
  Taking each eye in turn, she painted it
  Using a brush, a block of black, and spit.

At a Distance

If I could wrap my ghost about your acts,
Copy you with kisses more gentle than
A mirror's kisses in a darkened room,
I could be what you do and know your facts.

Nice work if we could get it. Not for us.
We take as consolation what we can.
I hear you talking in another room,
See what you can't: you, waiting for a bus.

But to be unsuspected skin between your skin
And the transparent wind that presses it!

We keep on wanting what we cannot win.

Mots d'Escalier

When I went up and found your note
I thought it worth the wait.
"Be back at half-past-eight," you wrote –
I've memorised those words by rote.
I lit a fag and hunched my coat
Around my shoulders. "It's a vote
Of confidence in her," I thought,
"I'll show her just how much I dote
On her, although she's late."

From half-past eight to nine o'clock
I sat upon your stair.
Remorselessly, tick-tock, tick-tock
The hands set off towards ten o'clock. . .
I picked my nose, I scratched my cock
And wondered should I take a rock
And wrap it in my woolly sock
And swing it, break the bloody lock
That kept me sitting there?

And then I wondered, "Is she dead
And lying in a ditch?
Or is it just her memory's fled
And she's forgotten what she said?
Or is she being wined and fed?
Or could it be that she's been led
Astray, the dozy featherhead
And lies in someone else's bed,
The faithless little bitch?"

Just then I heard your step outside
And saw you coming in.
I had one second to decide
Whether to greet with wounded pride
That cheery "Oh hello!" you cried.
I wanted to, I really tried,
But then I changed my mind. I lied
About my numb and frozen hide
And met you with a grin.

Okay. You win.

Curtains

For Claire

Net-nylon curtains, though they're not hand-made,
Not the real thing
(Ingenious machinery can copy-cat and bind
Miles every minute quickly on broad looms),
Still do as good a job in sunny rooms,
Scrawling their accidental runes of light and shade
On walls and writing paper, breakfast tray,
As if, in making them, some crone went blind.

To read their sprawl of curling pattern, thrown
Like something sung,
Set up an angled mirror, look in it and find
Your face tattooed with asymmetric lines
That crawl, slide as you turn your head; designs
Intended, surely, nowhere: now, here, shown
As loaded, coded messages, their play
As glancing-real as plates and bacon rind.

Where is that sun which flashed (Oh, who remembers when?),
Left us to hang
As overlapping shadows? That clever, left-behind
Machinery, getting on and getting laid, yes, that
Was hand-made, surely, but no better at
Communicating certainties. So, then,
Sad joy to see people in love: how they
Read nothing into shadows, wanting to be kind.

House-Sitting

For May Katzen

An empty house, though dense with other lives,
Mine for nine days. It comes complete
With central heating; bedding and a dog;
Money to pay the milkman; things to eat.

Not quite an Eden-freedom capsule. Dog
Must have her structured walks. We go
Around the arboretum well disguised:
I, as a burgher; she, as mine. We show

Equal delight (though I'm the more surprised)
The day a lovely friend explodes
Our settled new routine, lifts us away
By long, new roads to a beach and distant woods

Where we stroll free through an expansive day
And show, explore, engage. I note
The paddlers in that far blue line, the sea,
Look bigger, since I know they're people, than they ought.

That long-time fascination, constancy.

Next morning, dog and I come down, agree
That breakfast in a garden is all right,
And happiness is having learned, once more,
To know how big the roses are; to see, how bright.

An Elder Surprised

My friend's good friend, holding their naked son,
Came naked into the room. Giggles and all
The usual defensive banter came
Uneasily to my rescue in the game
That multiple degrees play lest they fall
Into some pit of feeling. All good fun.

In our perfect society, it's plain,
Committees have defined the right response
To beauty. Children can learn it at school.
Too old now, I suppose; can't learn; a fool.
How else could I, seeing them there, at once
Feel such a thief's delight, such welcome pain?

Night-Walks, Tyn Gwndwn

Olwen entices me, and so,
Although I'd thought I wouldn't go
We stroll downhill to Felinfach;
She makes a phone-call; we climb back.

After the spill of light at house and chapel,
The first few steps teach you to shorten step,
Entering a sightless under-cove: above, a cap
Of starless night-sky, just distinguishable.
To navigate in this you'll need half-sure
Guesses at hedgerow profiles, road-feel, echo-lore.

But then, surprisingly, the dark grows welcome. It
Insists you are unique, but lets you hear
Enough of other footsteps, giggles, dog-snuffs; fears
Give way to a sort of narrowing freedom, and the light
You reach at last by the school and the corner booth
Seems part, a pity; part banal; almost uncouth.

So, climbing back's a joy; and easier, for
This way, the sky's not black, though dark enough to bring
The fun of being, near enough, unseen, unseeing.
Now you can speak small truths into the darkness, or,
Feeling a small adventure near complete,
Become content with walking, silence, and no thought.

It's time for Harri's walk, and so,
Although I'd thought I wouldn't go.
We walk the dog to Felinfach.
I make a phone-call. We walk back.

Land's End

Where the land ends, the sea bends to the sky.
But is it fifteen miles or twenty-five,
The watcher on a cliff or six feet tall
Who shows – a dotted line leads from his eye –
Where the departing steamer's mast will dive
Into the shining out-of-sight? A small
Stiff drawing in a children's book that knew
One Thousand Things a Boy Could Make and Do.

So simple, then, to measure what could be
Seen with my open eyes. Now, I forget
The details of the rules I learnt to stow
The real world in my album. You could see
The dazzling place where seen and unseen met,
It said, by plain geometry. But now
Perspective grows uncertain, numbers lie,
The slow waves rise but never reach the sky.

Seen from the Train

Stopped for a moment. The rain has gone, has
Left behind a light so green and tolerant
The hillside and the houses angled there
Seem more than real. A supernatural
Ordinariness announces that tomorrow
We shall be older but, apart from that,
Nothing important will alter, nothing will move.

All on a level the bottom branches
Of trees, in open order in that meadow,
Will darken a plane six feet above the green;
In that far corner, porcupined with reeds,
A boggy dip will mark where pathways meet
And, in a silence deep as patience, farms
Unmanned and busy reach across the hills.

My train moves on and leaves me thinking how
It's most especially when they do not lie
Hardened by snapshot sunlight, these hills and fields,
Into flat tricks of light and shade
But, solid in dull air, retain their distances
They move me most. Moving, I make them wheel.

How still they'd be, if I could be so still.

A Nasty Moment

Cold field of cabbage heads, and each one wears
A wet, white, melting cap of morning frost.
Horrid to handle them, you think, glad that you're not
That gloomy tumbril-man, sack-caped, resentful,
Who surely must arrive to lop them off.

"How right you are to shudder," flaps
A single magpie, harbinger of sorrow,
And then, "Don't think that *you'll* escape." But wait;
What's that? Another bird was hiding, now
Winks grinning wings, erupts, subsides.
That's better. Two for joy.

Premature Retirement Prayer

O, my angelic uncles who
Have guarded me in dreams, appear;
Teach me to know what's mine to do;
Teach me to leave what isn't, to
Such others as stand near.

Striped shirt-sleeves rolled, hair by Brylcreem,
Pure common-sense in Sta-Prest pants,
I know you are not what you seem
And may appear, when women dream
As wily maiden aunts.

No matter: in whatever guise,
Keep me from posturing and puff
And when I reach for easy lies
Turn on me your reproachful eyes;
If I persist, get tough.

For that acknowledged lout, whose fart
Has made me blush, whose sweaty feet
Soiled all my socks, is losing heart;
He's getting ready to depart
And I'll share his defeat.

But if in that sad mansion, I
Am driven, by a maldesigned
Compulsion, to explore and pry,
Come smiling, shake your heads and sigh
So that I change my mind

And so behave myself that you
May oversee with smiles and praise
My tiny works, my prayers, my few
Good deeds, my petty crimes; renew
These extraordinary everydays.

Keep an Eye on Them

Furniture gets smaller as you get older.
What was once prison, house or cave becomes
Something to sit on, almost invisible. Oh, beware!
Neglect makes chairs grow sullen, tables mutter
That if they can't be submarines or sledges . . . well!
They're gathering now in the hallway, denser and malign,
Getting ready: getting ready to issue insulting demands
Which, sadly, you will have to honour.

Vacancies

I think about my life: two neutral scenes renew
Themselves, uncalled. North of the Harrow Road,
I'm walking, I think, to meet a friend. It's three
Or thereabouts, and Sunday afternoon. I'm on a broad
Avenue with a low wall one side; I can see
Over into a railway cutting. In the other scene, my view

Narrows to a long railing outside Regent's Park.
I trail along it. It's hot, I'm sweating, my feet
Hurt, but not badly: they've been worse. I don't
See a murder or crash in the cutting, or meet
God on the Outer Circle. There isn't
Anything special in either place: dust, sunlight, dark –

Green, iron railings, fallen leaves, a gable end.
It's nineteen fifty-three. In eighty-nine, these vacancies
Recur, dull-minted as the day I . . . what?
Not *lived* them, that's too strong. No, simply *was*
Inside them, passing through to something I forgot
From something I don't remember. That friend . . .

Karl? Or his wife, who made cartoon films? Gone,
    or more or less
– I wonder if all life will come to seem like this –
Sharply recalled for no good reason: puzzling, powerless.

Surviving

Light rain and freshening wind. Shoppers along
Our ageing, once-main road don't seem
To mind it, or not much: they mime
Vast shivering disgust, pull faces at
Their friends, then grin. Among
Them, pigeons grasp air, fanned feathers spread
Like fingers; sideslip in, peck up a shred
Of loot from someone's sandwich. It's the same

Grace that two kids on fat-tyre bikes display
Around my facing-forward stroll.
One scares me, though. I feel
Safer when he wheelies off, between
Two closing prams, and say,
"My God, these kids on bikes!" knowing I'll get
No argument among the pension set.
We stare at cabbage on an open stall.

A friend, to someone I don't know, reports:
"Oh, yes, you'd see her out on road . . .
Had a high colour . . . fell down dead!"
Hands flutter to her cheeks, to emphasise
High colour, gone. All sorts
Of vegetables occupy me: I
Heard all of it, yesterday, twice. The sky
Clears to what could be blue. A mad

Intense glare fixes me, from somewhere near
My knee: the child wears a green hat,
A badge marked "Woodstock," Para kit
In jungle camouflage. But then he puts
A finger in his ear,
Gapes up at Mum. She passes down a chip,
Well blown, to cool it, tested on her lip
For burn potential. I go home to start

Making the soup. Deciding how much green
To leave on leeks is a deep choice.
Scrub spuds, peel swede. Cube them. The space
All this takes up is automatic bliss.
The 'phone rings. Someone's seen
Something I ought to see on video.
We make a date. I tidy up and go
Out to the friends whose visit-day this is.

I leave before the pubs throw out. The road
Is light-points to infinity,
Which I reach soon enough, and go
Indoors to duties: gas-fire, blanket, kettle . . .
Familiar late-night mode.
Coat hung (that loop, must mend it, but who cares?)
And shoes kicked off, it's time for world affairs.
I find they've started. That old clock is slow.

Later, switch off the radio: the midnight list
Of money, menaces, excuse,
Horror and weather's done; a pause,
Then there's a small, internal, blipped full-stop
Inside the speakers, missed
Unless you listen for it. Now silence
Folds in around my dozy present-tense:
My day, thank God, unmentioned on the news.

Take One Answer

Meeting one's younger self, how think
"Well, now, and where –
Jersied monopolist, or
Winter-coated, belted –
Did your ten summers presence spring from?
Hey? You, over there?"

Without thinking, "And you?
Slow old size sixty,
So noticeably *breathing*,
Face like something melted,
So nothing I could ever be; and you?
Doing? What doing, there?"

The Ballad of the Sad Balloon

Denise, for my birthday, awarded me a mug
and a big balloon,
Red and rotund and overblown, like a rubbery
harvest moon.
And I hung it high on my living room wall, and it stayed
there week after week,
For she swore it was tied with a special knot that would
never let it leak.
And I thought it a sign that life would go on, the champagne
grow fizzier and fizzier –
But now . . . Eheu, rugosus est, Denisia, O Denisia.

Marked Changes

One of the perks, of course: when you come in
They do the usual stuff
With samples, blood and whatnot; bed you down
Into a way of doing things. The staff

Are kind and cheerful: death's not common here.
Soon you relax into
Undignified obedient clowning, hide your fear
Then, waking early, drag a curtain, view

From the ward window a road half-hidden under
A mute, unveiling sky
That does a Gypsy Rose Lee number on
A boundary fence, a pasture and some trees.

Something quite strange, out there, has happened to
The usual speed of light.
How can it change so slowly? Take that tree:
We knew it when it was a silhouette.

And now, by Early Pills, it's turned into
A dozen solid greens
Which nobody, for sure, saw born. And though
You could have stopwatch-counted cars, that line

Of nose-to-tailers sliding in to work
Grew quite unnoticed from
The early, lights-on loners. No, to mark
When changes happen you must use freeze-frame.

That's what they do, in here. You celebrate
So many red-star days,
From Nil-by-Mouth to Dinner on a Plate
And Sitting up at Table, on the way

To full adulthood – clothes, the taxi ride
That takes you outside, where
What little happens happens smoothly – you'd decide
This change-thing was enjoyable, only that, here,

You meet those old campaigners with thin grins
Who've done it all before
And count their change since last time, and begin
To know what no marked change is likely to restore.

In and Out

Raking a fire, November morning, out in the garden.
Fly from the embers, skirling upwards, black scraps of
        paper:
Yesterday's news.
Today the news is fog has invaded, year has hardened.

Along the saltings, commas that rise and spatter a vast
Grey nowhere are suddenly birds. Seen, they settle,
Beakily, you think,
Embarrassed, caught disturbing the year's first frost –

Which is, after all, only a warning; later it will be harder.

But, for the moment, riding past backs of houses,
How comforting to see, saffron in each dark block,
One lighted window.
Reliable men live there pursuing reliable courses

Which will take them, you can be sure, out from the
        unimportant
Secrets of half-awake bedrooms – knickers, dropped socks
        and, turning
Away from the light
With luxurious grumbles, wives who've forgotten they met –

Into this now. Before starting, on bikes with boxes
Wingnutted onto carriers, they'll pause and take the perk
Mortgaged days earn:
A moment to rake the roundel of embers, find an
        astonishing glow.

It has lasted, against the odds, all the time they slept.

Yesterday's news was bad, today's will be much better.
Left out in this gathering frost, the fire kept in;
It took so little.
Quick, rake it together; glittering nights are coming,

And longer ones, too, that will test banked timbers and
quell
Even the cheekiest birds until well past first light.
Simple lessons then:
Learn to be still, and moving. There you are out, and in.

Dao

Unthinking, find that you
Have left what you were at
And stand by the window
Offering no promise
To any strident voice.

Unlooking, stand before
Things pleasing to the sight.
Flower and leaf will grow
Without your comment. Night
Won't make them disappear.

Knowing nor good, nor harm,
Be without fear or charm.

Frontiers

Even for me, who never goes near one,
There is something disturbingly potent
About the notions that go with frontiers.

The movies help, of course, the stage-dressing
Of armed and neutral camps, between striped poles,
Where tired spies are swapped for tired spies.

And it has something to do with frontiers
That edge-of-town hotels are often known
for goings-on, straight faces and false names.

All that paraphernalia of passports
And men in boots and uniforms! But feeling
That when you pass one you have passed a test

Must come from something older – that you've done
Something vaguely illegal, though licensed,
And satisfied proper authority

That was quite right to stare at you so hard.
But, underneath all that, there's more: the sense
That even though frontiers grow usual

There's one remaining – somewhere in the North,
Most likely – and you'll come to it at night,
Half-way from maps to rumours, on a line

That the ice-bound train won't cross. Reaching it
You'll disembark, ignored by silent guards,
Discard your passport, duck beneath the poles. . . .

A Walk in the Evening

Look, it is raining over that ragged
Edge of the rising land.
Six fields step, clay-footed, across
The sodden trough between
Us and that merging.

To get there would be harder than it looks.

Behind us the house stands
Cowled in holly, laburnum, rhododendron.
Its windows gleam; it's still light here.
Later there'll be firelight in the kitchen,
And the smell of cooking.

To set out for the rain would be perverse.

We know, already, in that sough is
Nothing remarkable to find but
What we'd have left behind us:
Gutter cascades, wet greenery,
Houses and refuge.

And, if we did set out, who'd meet us
But half-embarrassed strangers? And,
Halfway across the fields, we'd lose the edge
In failing light or against
Further hills rising. . . .

Strange it should be so hard to turn away.

Only, that stubborn fidget to be moving
Hangs over us from childhood, when we could
Believe that falling band of grey was not
Rain but a more than natural event –
Like water rising up to meet the sky –
And, more, that when we reached it we would be
In it, yet see it as it looked from where
We saw it first. We know better now.

But all the same it's tempting. Who's for a walk?

"the poetry of Everyman"

Frank Redpath was born in Hull in 1927. He lived for some years in London, writing for children's comics, then returned with relief to Hull, where he taught at the College of Further Education. Jean Hartley of the Marvell Press says he had "a gift of laughter" and "an unusual talent for friendship." Endlessly patient and generous in his encouragement of young writers and artists, he was unambitious for himself except in craftsmanship. Redpath showed little interest in publication, but his poems appeared in magazines, in the Hull anthology *A Rumoured City* and in one book of his own, *To the Village* (Sonus Press, 1986). He was assembling a fuller collection, like this one, when he died in 1990.

"*A picture emerges of a kind of unillusioned idealism, ironic but romantic, gently anarchic, aware of the big picture, interpreting it through the particular and everyday.*" Sean O'Brien

"*That imaginative, spiritual feeling is often present in his work, as it should be in every poet's, but the gesture of his sharing it with his reader, his generosity, his openness, states simply that mystery and beauty are part of what it is to be alive. . . . In a poetry which is always lucid and accessible, these qualities assert it as more than sympathetic, social, or benevolent . . . as the poetry of Everyman.*" Douglas Dunn

"*The wonderful Frank Redpath.*" Letter to The Rialto